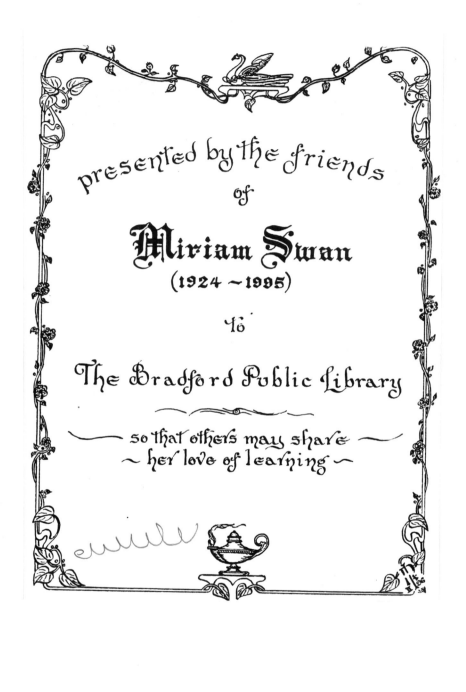

presented by the friends
of

Miriam Swan
(1924 ~ 1995)

to

The Bradford Public Library

— so that others may share —
~ her love of learning ~

TAIGA

APRIL PULLEY SAYRE

TWENTY-FIRST CENTURY BOOKS

A Division of Henry Holt and Company
• New York •

For Cathy, Lydia, and Rodney, my supportive siblings-in-law.
~A. P. S.~

ACKNOWLEDGMENTS

Thanks to the following scientists who reviewed portions of this manuscript and helped in research matters: Ken Winterberger, research forester at the USDA Forest Service in Alaska; and Jim C. Johnston, chief of New Park Proposals for Canada's North National Parks Systems Branch.

———————

Twenty-First Century Books
A Division of Henry Holt and Company, Inc.
115 West 18th Street
New York, NY 10011

Henry Holt ® and colophon are trademarks of
Henry Holt and Company, Inc.
Publishers since 1866

Library of Congress Cataloging-in-Publication Data
Sayre, April Pulley.
Taiga / April Pulley Sayre. —1st ed.
p. cm. — (Exploring earth's biomes)
Includes index.
1. Taiga ecology—Juvenile literature. 2.Taigas—Juvenile literature. 3. Taiga ecology—North America—Juvenile literature. 4.Taigas—North America—Juvenile literature. [1. Forest ecology. 2. Forests and forestry. 3. Ecology.] I. Title. II. Series: Sayre, April Pulley. Exploring earth's biomes.
QH541.5.T3S28 1994   574.5'2642—dc20
                                                            94–19388
ISBN 0–8050–2830–7
First Edition—1994

Printed in the United States of America
All first editions are printed on acid–free paper ∞.

10 9 8 7 6 5 4 3 2 1

Photo Credits
p. 8: Charlie Ott/Photo Researchers, Inc.; p. 14: Michael Giannechini/Photo Researchers, Inc.; p. 18: April Pulley Sayre; p. 24: U.S. Department of the Interior, Glacier National Park; p. 25: Tom Bean; p. 29: Bruce M. Herman/Photo Researchers, Inc.; p. 29 (inset): Helen Williams/Photo Researchers, Inc.; p. 31: Stouffer Productions/Animals Animals; p. 32: Alan Carey/Photo Researchers, Inc.; p. 35: John Warden/Alaska Stock Images; p. 41: Rod Planck/Photo Researchers, Inc.; p. 50: Bobbie Kingsley/Photo Researchers, Inc.; p. 55: Jeff Schultz/Alaska Stock Images.

CONTENTS

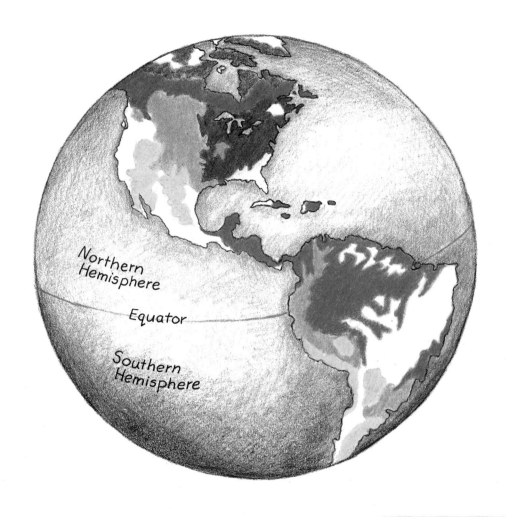

Northern
Hemisphere

Equator

Southern
Hemisphere

rain forest
grassland
desert
temperate deciduous forest
taiga
tundra

INTRODUCTION

Take a look at the earth as a whole and you'll see its surface can be divided into living communities called biomes. Desert, rain forest, tundra, taiga, temperate deciduous forest, grassland, and polar desert are some of the main terrestrial biomes—biomes on land. Each biome has particular kinds of plants and animals living in it. Scientists also identify other biomes not mentioned here, including aquatic biomes—biomes of lakes, streams, and the sea.

When their boundaries are drawn on a globe, terrestrial biomes look like horizontal bands stacked up from Pole to Pole. Starting from the equator and moving outward toward the Poles, you'll find rain forests, grasslands, deserts, and grasslands once again. Then things change a little. The next biomes we think of—temperate deciduous forests, taiga, and tundra—exist only in the Northern Hemisphere. Why is this true? Well, if you look in the Southern Hemisphere, you'll see there's very little land in the regions where these biomes would supposedly lie. There's simply nowhere for these biomes to exist! Conditions on small pieces of land—islands and peninsulas—that lie in these areas are greatly affected by sea conditions and are very different from those on continents.

But why do biomes generally develop in these bands? The answer lies in the earth's climate and geology. Climate is affected by the angle at which sunlight hits the earth. At the equator, sunlight passes through the atmosphere and hits the earth straight on, giving it its full energy. At the Poles, sunlight must pass through more atmosphere and it hits the earth at an angle, with less energy per square foot. Other factors also influence where biomes lie: the bands of rising and falling air that circulate around the planet; the complex weather systems created by jutting mountains, deep valleys, and cold currents; the glaciers that have scoured the lands in years past; and the activities of humans. These make biome boundaries less regular than the simplified bands described above.

1
THE TAIGA BIOME

The taiga is a good place for fairy tales and wild imaginings. On a spring morning, dark evergreens, their branches heavy with needles, give off a sweet fragrance. Birds' watery whistles echo among the trees. Soft moss and fallen tree needles invite you to lie down and take a nap—perhaps even a 20-year nap like fairy tale character Rip Van Winkle. But the cold, crisp air in this northern forest is likely to keep you walking, just to stay warm.

On your walk you may hear flocks of boreal chickadees chattering in the trees, or red squirrels noisily chewing on pine seeds. With a little detective work you may discover signs of other animals as well. Scratch marks on a tree reveal where a bear has sharpened its claws. Small, brown, egg-shaped pellets indicate a larger forest traveler was here before you, and left its calling card: moose droppings.

Moose are a frequent sight among the taiga conifers—the cone-bearing trees common to this region. Their presence among the spruce trees has even led some people to nickname taiga the "spruce–moose" forest. But taiga contains not just spruce, but many other trees such as pine, fir, tamarack, birch, alder, and aspen.

Like rain forests, deserts, and tundra, taiga is a biome—a geographic area that has a certain kind of climate and a certain kind of community of plants and animals. The largest terrestrial—land—biome on earth, taiga stretches in a band across the northern parts of North America, Europe,

Taiga, or boreal forest, is a vast, wild biome found in the northern part of three continents.

and Asia, covering about 50 million acres (20 million hectares) in all. It is located generally south of the tundra, but north of the temperate deciduous forests and temperate grasslands.

Northern winds help make the taiga snow-covered and cold for most of the year, roughly from October to May. During its brief summer, however, the taiga can be cool and moist at times, hot and humid at others.

Scientists still debate over what exactly to call this biome. Some prefer the Russian term *taiga*, others call it northern coniferous forest, while still others call it the boreal forest.

No matter what you call it, this biome is a wondrous place. Its acres of evergreen trees are home to great gray owls, mushrooms of many colors, and elusive wolverines— fierce predators rarely seen even by the scientists who study them. Scattered in the forest's midst are wetlands: lakes, ponds, and moss-covered bogs that support beaver, fish, water birds, and strange, insect-eating pitcher plants. And preserved deep in its peat moss bogs are ancient secrets: the pollen of plants and even the bodies of people who lived thousands of years ago.

TYPES

There are two main types of taiga:
- Open, lichen woodland, which has trees spaced far apart, with lichen growing in between them.
- Closed forest, which has trees close together, and a shaded, often moss-covered forest floor.

TEMPERATURES

Daytime air temperature changes drastically throughout the year, but not day to day.
- Average yearly temperature range: -65°F to 30°F (-54°C to -1°C) in winter and 20°F to 70°F (-7°C to 21°C) in summer.
- At times summer temperatures may get up in the 80s°F (high 20s°C)!
- The average temperature is below freezing for six months of the year.

WEATHER

- Winters are cold with some snowfall. Summers can be warm and rainy.
- Average humidity is high in summer, from 50 to 80 percent. The air is much drier in winter.
- Most of the precipitation arrives as rain in summer.
- Average yearly precipitation: 12 to 33 inches (30 to 84 centimeters).

SOIL

- Taiga soils vary tremendously. Many are geologically young and poorly developed. They tend to be acidic and either nutrient poor or have nutrients unavailable to plants because the soil is so cold.
- Decomposition of organic materials—dead plants and

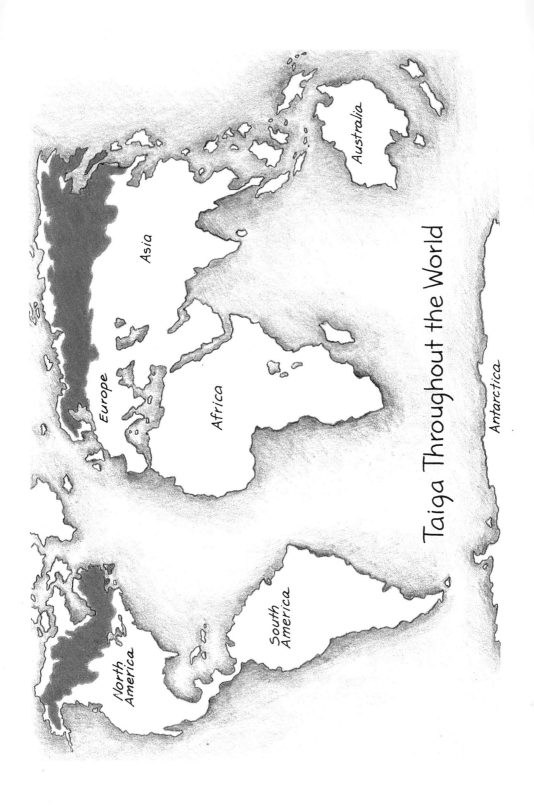

Taiga Throughout the World

animals—is slow. As a result, thick layers of undecayed vegetation build up on the forest floor.

PLANTS

- Biomass—the total weight of plant matter—for a given area of the taiga is not as high as in tropical and deciduous forests.
- The taiga has fewer tree species than other forest biomes such as tropical rain forests and temperate deciduous forests.
- Evergreen, coniferous trees such as spruce, fir, and pine dominate much of the forest, although larch—a deciduous conifer—dominates Siberian taiga.
- Broad-leafed, deciduous trees, such as birch, balsam poplar, and aspen also make up a significant part of the taiga, especially in southern regions.

ANIMALS

- Taiga has fewer animal species than forests such as tropical rain forest and temperate deciduous forest. It has a low species diversity.
- Many birds from the tropics migrate to the taiga to nest in summer.
- Taiga animal population size rises and falls dramatically, sometimes in cycles.
- Birds, mammals, and insects are common. Amphibians and reptiles are scarce.

2
TAIGA IN NORTH AMERICA

Stretching across central Alaska, the bulk of Canada, and the northern reaches of the lower 48 states, the North American taiga is a vast forest of conifers, dominated by white spruce, black spruce, balsam fir, and tamarack. Yet the taiga is not an unbroken expanse of green forest; it's a patchwork of many habitats. Snaking through the forests are streams and rivers, where salmon swim and willows grow. And dotting the landscape are wet spots: lakes, bogs, and ponds, where you might find moose feeding on aquatic plants, mink frolicking along the water's edge, or cranberries growing in abundance.

In northern Canada the taiga gradually tapers off, and the Arctic tundra—a cold, treeless biome characterized by low-growing plants—begins. This transition area, where taiga and tundra overlap, is called the forest–tundra ecotone. (In Alaska, the transition between taiga and tundra is more abrupt, with little forest–tundra.) In southern Canada, taiga mingles with temperate deciduous forests in some places, and in some areas with prairie. On the western coast of Canada and the southeast coast of Alaska, wet coastal weather favors the growth of tall coniferous forests called temperate rain forest, instead of taiga.

Flying over the North American taiga, you can identify two distinctive types of taiga: closed forest and lichen woodland. Closed forest taiga is made up of many closely

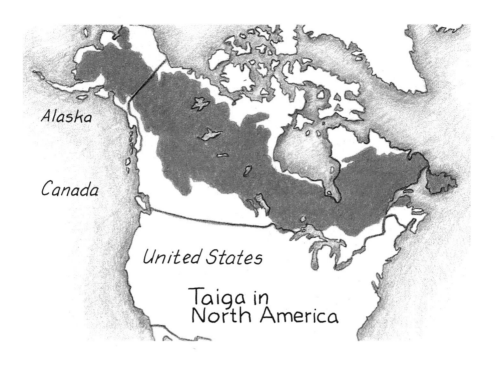

Taiga in
North America

spaced trees, often with moss covering the ground. Lichen woodland taiga, which has trees spaced farther apart and lichen covering much of the ground, is more common in the northern taiga, or at high altitudes in the southern taiga.

Overall, North America's taiga has much in common with taiga in the rest of the world. Like the Siberian taiga in Russia and Asia, North American taiga has coniferous trees, an abundance of moss, a short growing season, and long, cold winters. Some of the tree species are the same, or closely related, although Siberia's forests often have taller trees. Perhaps most surprising, many animal species, such as the moose, lynx, bear, and great gray owl, are found throughout the taiga worldwide.

Despite the characteristics it shares with taiga all over the world, North America's taiga nevertheless has its own regional flavor. Some of its remarkable features are described below:

*Moose—the largest member of the deer family—are abundant
in the taiga.*

- Covering 17,300 square miles (27,900 kilometers), Wood
  Buffalo National Park, Canada's largest park, contains
  wide expanses of taiga, where wood bison—also called
  wood buffalo—live. These forest-dwelling bison are larger
  and darker than the bison that used to roam North
  America's prairies in great numbers. But they are the
  same species. Whooping cranes, bears, beavers, muskrats,
  and moose also live in the park.
- In Canada's Northwest Territories, at Great Slave Lake, a
  lake dotted with many islands, geologists have found
  granite more than two billion years old. These rocks are
  some of the oldest rocks found on earth.
- The name of Alaska's Denali National Park and Preserve
  comes from the Athabascan Indian word, *Denali*, meaning "the high one" or "the great one." Denali is the Indian
  name for Mt. McKinley, the highest peak in North
  America, which is located in the park. It is surrounded by
  both taiga and alpine tundra.

3
TAIGA WEATHER, CLIMATE, AND GEOLOGY

Dotted with lakes and bogs, the taiga is, in many ways, a wet biome. Yet it doesn't receive very much precipitation. So why is it wet? The answer, in short, is cold weather. Cold temperatures in the region slow evaporation. Precipitation that does arrive stays. In some areas a layer of frozen ground called permafrost also prevents water from draining away. As a result, water "puddles up" over the permafrost layer and the rock layer, forming wet features such as lakes, bogs, and muskegs.

TAIGA WEATHER

On a summer vacation to the taiga, be prepared for cool *or* hot weather. Summer temperatures are mostly cool, averaging 20°F to 70°F (-7°C to 21°C). But sometimes afternoon temperatures can reach into the 80s°F (high 20s°C) and the moist forest can feel downright muggy. In spring, fall, or winter, it's best to be prepared for snow and cold. Winter temperatures in the taiga range from -65°F to 30°F (54°C to -1°C). Frostbite and hypothermia—dangerously low body temperature—can be a serious concern.

Snow, Snow, Snow Snow boots, skis, and snowshoes all come in handy for taiga travel most of the year. The taiga receives 12 to 33 inches (30 to 85 centimeters) of precipitation per year on average. That precipitation arrives mostly as rain in summer, but also as snow in winter. The taiga may only receive a foot or a few feet of snow in the winter, but because of consistently cold temperatures, the snow builds up, instead of melting between storms. In fact, snow cover lasts nine months of the year in northern parts of the taiga! Over the course of the winter, the piled-up snow can change in structure, creating a brittle layer called depth hoar that collapses underfoot, making it difficult to travel except on established trails.

Long Winter Nights, Long Summer Days   Because of its position relatively near the North Pole, the taiga experiences long, dark nights in winter and long, sunlit days in summer. At the taiga's northern reaches, the sun may skirt the horizon but never actually set for days in the summer. While in winter the sun may not rise above the horizon for days or weeks. Day length varies from north to south within

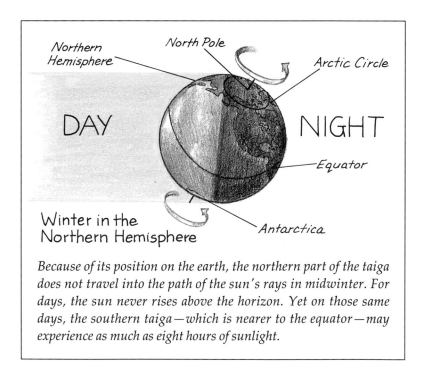

Because of its position on the earth, the northern part of the taiga does not travel into the path of the sun's rays in midwinter. For days, the sun never rises above the horizon. Yet on those same days, the southern taiga—which is nearer to the equator—may experience as much as eight hours of sunlight.

the taiga. A long summer day at the northern reaches of the taiga may last 24 hours, while the longest summer day in the southern taiga may only have 16 hours of daylight.

TAIGA BORDERS

The taiga biome stretches in a broken band around the earth, just below the Arctic, in an area called the subarctic. The taiga's borders are two isotherms. Isotherms are boundaries that depend on yearly temperature. Generally, taiga grows in areas north of the July 65°F (18°C) isotherm, meaning the average temperature for the month of July is not over 65°F (18°C). Taiga grows south of the July 55°F (13°C) isotherm. These isotherms are only general guidelines. Scientists still debate exactly what taiga is and where it is located. In places, the taiga spills over or does not reach these isotherms because other factors influence its existence. Precipitation, soil, permafrost, topography, and past history also influence the taiga's boundaries.

A LAND SHAPED BY ICE

Eighteen thousand years ago, where Canada's taiga is today, ice was piled high, in places a mile thick! During the last ice age, great rivers of ice, called glaciers, moved down over Canada, parts of Alaska, and the northern portion of the lower 48 states.

When the earth's climate finally warmed, and the ice melted, it revealed a land almost bare of soil. The weight of the ice, pushing along the continent, had scraped soil and forest off the land, ground rock into pieces, and gouged giant holes in the landscape. It took thousands of years for soil to develop and forests to become reestablished. But eventually taiga trees and plants that had survived in large unglaciated regions—south of the ice, and in central Alaska and Canada's Yukon—reseeded the newly revealed lands. Taiga now grows on a variety of terrain, on mountains,

Although they are mere leftovers from a much colder, icier time, glaciers are still one of nature's most impressive sights.

rolling hills, flatlands, and near water features such as streams, rivers, waterfalls, and lakes.

Today, although the large glaciers are gone, evidence of their action remains. Ridges of rubble, sharp cliffs, rounded boulders, holes, pits, and scrape marks on rocks are all signs of glacial action. The lakes and ponds scattered across Canada's landscape are also glacial remnants, formed when water filled up large pits carved out by glaciers. Even places such as interior Alaska and parts of Siberia, which were not covered by ice during the last ice age, nevertheless show some effects of nearby glacial activity. After the glaciers retreated, loess—a type of fine silt created by glaciers—was deposited by rivers and wind on these lands.

SOILS: YOUNG, SHALLOW, AND COLD

As a result of its glacial history, most of the taiga's soil is young. It hasn't had time to develop the deep, thick layers of fertile soil present in the temperate deciduous forest and tallgrass prairie. Such soil development progresses slowly in cold climates. As a result, taiga soils are thin and not very good for farming. Even if the soil has the minerals plants need, it's so cold that plants can't use much of this mineral content. (At low soil temperatures, the plants can't efficiently carry out the chemical reactions needed to absorb minerals.)

Leached Soil   In some places if you pull up the mosses, or brush away the dead evergreen tree needles on the forest floor of the taiga, you'll find a layer made up of interwoven roots, fungi, and other materials. Underneath this layer is white or gray soil that is mineral poor. Natural acids from the evergreen needles wash down through this layer, leaching, or carrying away organic particles, minerals, and clay. These particles deposit in a reddish layer below. This kind of soil, called podzol, or spodosol, is common in cool, moist biomes such as taiga. But the taiga has other types of soil, varying from the spodosol to a thin dusting of loess over bedrock. What do taiga soils have in common? In short, they're all shallow, cold, and not very old.

Piles upon Piles   To keep food from spoiling, people put it in a refrigerator or freezer. That's similar to what happens on the floor of the taiga. Temperatures there are cool much of the year, so the organisms that break down material into soil aren't very active. Leaves and moss are also acidic and remain waterlogged, which slows down decay. As a result, the taiga's organic material does not decompose quickly; it piles up. This means the nutrient wealth of the forest is tied up in a thick layer of dead vegetation on the forest floor, where it is unavailable to trees and other plants for use in growth. This layer of vegetation is not considered part of the soil.

Frozen Ground   Some parts of the taiga have permafrost. In summer, the upper layer of this permafrost may melt, creating a layer called the active layer, where biological activity can take place. But in general, permafrost makes it difficult for plants to root deep into the soil. Freezing and thawing of permafrost can also crack and damage roots. And each year, as the ground melts and refreezes, pockets of ice and air within it shift. This thrusting up and down creates lumpy ground.

THE BIG PICTURE, AND
THE LITTLE PICTURE WITHIN

Climatic conditions experienced by plants and animals within the taiga depend on more than weather. They depend on the structure of the forest itself. Leafy tree branches shield a rabbit from chilling winds. A tree's shade keeps soil cool, and snow from melting. A fallen leaf, a rock, a hill, a mushroom—any of these things can create pockets within the forest that are warmer, colder, shadier, or less windy than the rest of the forest. These little pockets with different conditions are called microclimates. In many ways these microclimates are as important to the survival of plants and animals as the overall climate—the macroclimate—of the whole taiga biome.

TAIGA PLANTS

In a land where growing seasons are short, there's little time for a tree to grow new leaves each spring. In the taiga, where both available soil nutrients and growing time are scarce, growing a whole new set of leaves each year is doubly difficult. No wonder most taiga tree species are evergreens. They keep their leaves for more than one season. Being evergreen is just one of many strategies plants have evolved to survive the taiga's harsh climate. From waxy needles to fungi partners to cones that drop seeds after forest fires, taiga plants have an amazing array of adaptations.

TREE ADAPTATIONS

The most common trees in the taiga—the conifers—have neither flowers nor fruits. In late winter or early spring, they form two kinds of cones: cones that have pollen and cones that are fertilized by wind-blown pollen. Pollen blows from tree to tree, fertilizing the cones. Once a cone is fertilized, it grows larger, and its seeds develop under tightly closed scales. When the seeds are ripe, and the cone dries out, it opens. Each seed spins on a tiny flattened wing, away from the plant, and to the ground where it can sprout. Many seeds, however, will never take this first flight. Millions become food for hungry squirrels, who rip apart the cones and eat the seeds, leaving behind piles of reddish cone scales on the ground.

Conifer Clones   Some conifers can reproduce another way—by layering. Layering occurs when snow or debris weighs down a lower branch, which becomes covered with soil. Where it contacts the soil, this branch forms roots, and can grow into a new tree, similar to the way a gardener takes cuttings of a plant and roots them. Unlike trees grown from seeds, trees grown by layering are clones. Clones are genetically identical to the original tree.

Needles Are Leaves   Conifers have needles instead of broad leaves. Long, thin, wax-covered needles lose less water, retain more heat, and shed snow more easily than broad leaves. It's fairly obvious why a tree in such a cold climate would need to retain heat and shed snow. But why conserve water? Because rain may fall on branches and never reach tree roots. And most important of all, cold temperatures make it difficult for trees to absorb what water is present in the environment. So, any water they lose can cause trouble. One taiga conifer, the tamarack, has an additional adaptation that fights winter dehydration. It drops its needles in fall; that way it doesn't lose any water through its needles in winter.

Hold on Tight   Taiga conifers, except for the tamarack, keep their leaves in winter. A spruce may keep its needles for 15 years, while other species may keep theirs for only 2 or 3 years. Evergreen trees lose their needles only a few at a time, gradually, so the loss may not be noticeable. In contrast, broad-leaf taiga trees such as birch, balsam poplar, and aspen shed their leaves all at once, in fall. These trees, as well as the tamarack, are considered deciduous. They regrow their leaves in the spring.

Drop 'Em or Keep 'Em?   Both evergreen and deciduous lifestyles have their advantages. Deciduous trees, by shedding their leaves, use less energy during winter, and don't run the risk of snow and ice building up on their leaves and breaking their branches. Evergreen trees, by keeping their leaves, don't have to grow a whole new set of leaves at the start of the next growing season. But they do risk snow buildup and branch breakage. This is one reason conifer trees are cone-shaped, with branches that droop downward to help them shed snow.

Shallow Roots   Looking at a fallen taiga tree, you can see its roots form a wide, shallow mat. That's just as well, because taiga soils are shallow, usually not more than 10 inches (25 centimeters) deep. Deeper roots would have a hard time penetrating permafrost and could absorb only a small amount of nutrients because the permafrost is so cold.

Winterizing and Frostbite   To survive long, cold, snowy winters, taiga trees winterize. In fall, they slow the chemical processes going on in their tissues.They also undergo a process called hardening, which makes them more resistant to freezing. A spruce tree's needles, which in summer can only tolerate a temperature above 19°F (-7°C), can tolerate temperatures as low as -40°F (-40°C) after hardening. Occasionally, however, a cold frost comes in early fall, before the trees harden, or late in spring, after trees have lost their cold-tolerance. Cold snaps such as these can cause frostbite, freezing new leaves, killing off young shoots, or freezing bark tissue, which later forms scars.

Fire Survivors   Fire is a recurring event in the taiga, so many taiga trees are adapted to it. Thick bark protects some trees from mild, low-heat fires. Many broad-leafed trees resprout from a trunk or root undamaged by the fire. Most conifers, however, can't. But they can reseed an area. Black spruce, jack pine, and lodgepole pine have cones held high on the tree. Even if fire moves through the forest, some of

Fire provides the right conditions for lodgepole pinecones to open and drop their seeds.

the cones on high branches may survive. The heat of the fire makes the cones open and the seeds drop to the ground to reseed the forest floor.

TREES THAT "POLLUTE"

If you walk into the taiga, you can smell it almost right away—that sweet, pleasant, pungent smell of conifers. Many people associate this smell with Christmas trees, which are sometimes spruce or fir. The smell comes from a kind of natural air pollution—an oily resin called terpene made by conifers. Droplets of this resin can create a bluish haze in the air. The Blue Ridge Mountains of Virginia and the Great Smoky Mountains of Tennessee and North Carolina got their names from this haze. Spruce and fir grow on these mountains, although they are not part of the taiga. Those mountains are mostly clothed in temperate deciduous forest.

Resin from taiga conifers creates a wonderfully sweet, fresh smell.

LIFE IN THE NEIGHBORHOOD

A tree in the taiga is not alone. A host of plants, fungi, and animals live in, on, and around it every day. Some of these neighbors help the tree to grow, others can weaken or kill it, and still others exist nearby, yet do little to affect the tree's growth overall.

Forest Structure   Coniferous trees are not the only plants in the taiga. Broad-leafed trees such as birch, aspen, and cottonwood grow in certain spots, particularly in burned-over areas. Willows, too, can in some places reach tree size. Underneath taiga trees, small herbs, mushrooms, lichens, and mosses grow. And wherever enough sunlight enters the forest, shrub thickets of blueberries, willows, alders and other plants thrive.

Fungi "Friends"   Like the trees in many biomes, the taiga's conifers have fungi "partners" to help them get nutrients from the soil. Mycorrhizal fungi, which look like tiny hairs, grow outward from the conifer's roots. They help the roots to absorb the water and minerals needed for photosynthesis. In return for this "service," fungi receive a portion of the food that conifers make. Scientists call this kind of partnership mutualism. Mutualism is a relationship in which each organism benefits from the other.

Ghostly Indian Pipes   Growing at the base of many coniferous trees are white, translucent plants shaped like pipes with their stems in the ground. These plants have neither typical leaves nor the green chlorophyll that helps most plants make food. Indian pipe and two related plants—pine drops and pine sap—get their food from their roots, which attract mycorrhizal fungi. The same mycorrhizal fungi that grow intermingled with tree roots intertwine with the Indian pipe's roots and feed it, so the Indian pipe gets nourishment indirectly from the tree. Indian pipes, pine drops, and pine sap may also get food from remains of dead organisms in the soil.

Fungus "Amongus"   Not just mycorrhizae, but many types of fungi are abundant in the taiga. And that mushroom growing up from the ground or the bracket fungus sticking out like a shelf from a tree, is only a tiny fraction of the entire fungal organism. Fungi grow in trees and underground, stretching out over many square yards, in networks of strands called hyphae. The mushroom stem and cap, or the bracket fungus "shelf," is a structure the fungus uses to reproduce. It's something like what a seed pod is for a plant. Spores fall out from underneath the shelf or cap, and fall or blow to new sites. Most fungi grow on dead trees, helping to decompose the wood tissue. But some fungi attack living trees.

Insects, Insects, Insects   Some taiga plants have tannins and other toxins in their leaves to discourage leaf eaters. Yet insects are still big consumers of trees. Acres of trees may be partly defoliated—stripped of many of their leaves—in a single season by insects such as the spruce budworm or the larch sawfly. Repeated attacks by insects, year after year, can kill a tree or weaken it, causing it to die from other causes, such as an early freeze, or a fungus.

SEASONS OF THE TAIGA

In a temperate deciduous forest, trees mark the four seasons of the year—spring, summer, winter, fall—in dramatic ways. Not so in the taiga. Even in the middle of winter, most taiga trees are still green, with their leaves intact, though perhaps snow-covered. In spring, temperate deciduous forests burst with spring wildflowers growing in the light shining through tree branches bare of leaves. But in the taiga, most trees still have their leaves, so wildflowers on the forest floor are shaded even in spring. They do not experience the growth spurt common in temperate deciduous forests.

Fall is when the leaves of temperate deciduous forest trees turn color and drop. The taiga undergoes more subtle changes in autumn. Large expanses of the taiga are dominated by evergreen trees, whose leaves remain green even as they slow down their chemical processes for winter. Yet taiga still exhibits a bit of a fall show. The needles of tamarack trees turn brown and drop. The leaves of many shrubs and bog plants turn deep red. And broad-leafed, deciduous forest trees, such as aspen and birch, turn gold and drop their leaves. They echo the more dramatic, widespread changes that occur in temperate deciduous forests.

5
TAIGA ANIMALS

To get to know taiga animals—their habits, their patterns, their lives—walk in the taiga after a snowstorm. You may only see a few animals, but the tracks you'll find in the snow can often tell you a lot about the life of the forest. Pawprints indicate where a rabbit ran and a lynx followed. Feather-shaped etchings mark the spot where a raven landed to feed on a carcass. And deep pits reveal where caribou dug for lichen. Obviously, even in winter, this forest is alive—with squirrels, bears, deer, moose, martens, wolverines, and other wild creatures.

SURVIVING THE WINTER:
MIGRATION AND HIBERNATION

Cold, snow, and the scarcity of food in winter are central facts of life for taiga animals. To survive these difficult conditions, some animals avoid the winter season entirely by migrating to warmer climates. Others stay put and cope, remaining fully active. Still others hibernate to lessen the effects of the harsh taiga climate on their bodies.

Migration   Of the 300 bird species that live in the taiga in summer, only 30 species stay for the winter. The rest are summer visitors who leave in the fall, migrating as far south as South America. Why do millions of birds travel thousands of miles to the taiga each year? Insects! Like the tundra, the taiga has a summer abundance of insects. The forest

Migrating Canada geese, flying in their V-shaped formations, are seen during spring and fall in North American skies.

is alive with beetles, larch sawflies, spruce budworms, and hordes of flies and mosquitoes. In summer, flycatchers grab insects in midair. Woodpeckers, red-breasted nuthatches, boreal chickadees, and golden-crowned kinglets patrol tree trunks, snatching insect larvae from bark crevices. Boreal forests also provide birds with a good place to raise young, with generally more space and less competition with other birds than in tropical and temperate forests.

It's for the Birds   Other taiga animals, such as butterflies, caribou, and salmon, also migrate. Salmon return to the streams where they were born in order to reproduce. In fall, caribou walk from the tundra to the taiga, where they stay the winter. However, such large-scale migrations are not as common among mammals as among birds. It takes more energy to walk than to fly such long distances.

Hibernation   To survive the winter, animals such as arctic ground squirrels curl up in dens or under the snow and

29

enter a metabolic state called hibernation. To hibernate, they become sluggish or motionless, their body functions are reduced, and their body temperature is lowered, close to freezing. By hibernating during winter, animals save energy and have a better chance of surviving until spring when food is more plentiful.

A Bear of a Question   For many years scientists disagreed over whether bears hibernated or not. Bears don't eat, drink, or urinate during their three to six months in a winter den, but scientists weren't sure bears were inactive enough, with a low enough body temperature to qualify as true hibernators. To study this question, scientists went into bears' dens during winter to measure the bears' temperatures. Unfortunately, this involves using not a mouth thermometer, but one for the other end. Several scientists chased out of bears' dens discovered the overwintering bears aren't as "out of it" as they once thought!

It turns out that during their winter denning period, the bears' heart rates slow and their temperatures are lower than normal, but are not near freezing, as in most hibernators. Bears even give birth and nurse young during this period. Unlike other hibernators, they can wake up fairly quickly. That is why, although scientists once thought bears' winter state was kind of "shallow" hibernation, most now agree that it doesn't qualify as hibernation at all.

OTHER WAYS TO COPE

Cold, heavy, and thick, snow blankets the winter taiga, making it difficult for some animals to travel to reach the foods they need to survive. But snow has its good points; in fact, it's the key to winter survival for many animals. Voles, weasels, and arctic hares tunnel down into the snow to keep warm. Just 10 inches (25 centimeters) under the blanket of snow, the temperature remains fairly constant, around 32°F (0°C).

Crystal Tunnels   In winter, there's a crystalline world under the snow, where shrews scamper, voles snooze, and mice nibble on seeds and grasses they have stored. This is depth hoar—the bottommost layer of snow. It forms when summer warmth, trapped in the ground, melts some of the winter snow closest to the ground. Melting, dripping, then refreezing, the snow forms a sort of crystal palace—open spaces interspersed with "columns" made of ice and snow. Several inches thick, this layer allows small mammals to stay active within its warm spaces. At times, however, the breath of these animals creates a toxic buildup of carbon dioxide. To alleviate this problem, the rodents dig ventilation shafts to the surface for air.

Super Snowshoes   To walk on deep snow, people use snowshoes, which distribute their weight over a large area so they don't sink deeply with each step. Animals have their

Do not to disturb a bear in its winter den—it's likely it hasn't eaten in months!

*Neither the arctic hare nor the lynx has the
advantage in a chase, since both have natural "snowshoes"
that help keep them from sinking in deep snow.*

own natural "snowshoes." The broad, furry paws of arctic
hares distribute their weight over the snow so they can run
across it. Because they are able to walk on top of the deep
snow, arctic hares can reach the tender tops of willow
branches, which serve as food. But these hares need to stay
alert! Lynx, who hunt them, also have broad, furry paws that
enable them to chase down hares on hard-packed snow.

MAKE TRACKS!

To know the forest and its animals, especially in winter,
learn to track—to recognize the pawprints, hoofprints, claw
marks, and scat (droppings) left by animals.

To familiarize yourself with tracks and tracking, con-
sult the following books:

- *A Field Guide to Mammal Tracking in North America* by James
  Halfpenny (Boulder: Johnson Books, 1986).

• *Tom Brown's Field Guide to Nature Observation & Tracking* by Tom Brown, Jr., with Brandt Morgan (New York: Berkley, 1983).

Then try these activities:

A. Track Experiments

Find or clear an area of dirt in your yard or somewhere nearby. This will be your tracking pit. Press a shoe or your bare foot in the dirt to make a track. Six hours later, make an identical impression with your shoe or foot beside the original one. Then look at the first track. How does it look six hours since it was made? Is it as deep, as distinct? Record your observations. The next day, add more tracks to the tracking pit and see how the earlier ones have changed. Has it rained? Has it been windy? How do these and other weather conditions change the track? Create your own experiments to teach yourself how tracks change with age and weather conditions.

B. Plaster Casts of Tracks

If you find a track and you want to preserve it, you can make a sketch of it, or you can make a plaster cast. Mix up a small quantity of plaster of Paris, according to the directions on the package. Pour the thin liquid into the track until it flows over the edges slightly. Let the plaster dry and carefully lift out the cast. Use the plaster cast for your studies.

Now that you're learning tracks, keep an eye out for them all the time. Look in soft mud, in sand, or in snow to see what track stories you can find.

Changing Coat Color Weasels, snowshoe hares, and ptarmigans change from a brown color in summer and fall to white in winter. At first glance, this adaptation seems like a clear-cut case of animal camouflage—animals trying to fit in with their surroundings. After all, the brown fits in with the summer colors, and white is almost invisible against the snow. Having a color that matches the background helps prey hide from predators and predators sneak up on prey.

However, the reason for this coloring may not be so simple after all. It may have as much to do with staying warm as staying hidden. Colored animals have the pigment melanin inside their feathers or fur. But white hairs have no melanin, just air-filled spaces, where the pigment would be. These pockets of air help insulate animals, keeping them warm in winter.

GETTING A MEAL

Spruce grouse prefer eating insects, seeds, and easy-to-digest plant parts in the summer months. But in winter, these dappled, chickenlike birds will even eat spruce needles to get the nutrition they need. It's adaptations such as these that help animals obtain food year-round.

Seedy Characters   Red squirrels, pine siskins, red grosbeaks, and crossbills rely on the taiga's abundant conifer seeds for food. The awkward-looking crossed bill of the crossbill is actually a handy tool for prying apart spruce cones. The bird pokes its beak in between cone scales, then closes it, so its beak tips push apart the cone scales. Then the bird can use its tongue to reach the seeds underneath the scales. To survive the long winter, squirrels store piles of conifer seeds inside or at the base of trees. They even gather and dry mushrooms for their winter food cache.

Woodier Tastes   It may be hard to believe, but bark and wood are also popular food items. It's not uncommon to see a moose reaching up to pull down poplar branches, or browsing on willow shoots by a river. Beavers eat bark, small shoots, and branches of trees. And in winter, porcupines nibble on tree bark. But then again, these prickly creatures aren't known for their discriminating tastes. They've been caught gnawing on power lines, park signs, ax handles, and even car tires and steering wheels!

Taiga Predators   Taiga is home to a variety of predatory mammals, including foxes, wolves, wolverines, weasels, lynx, martens, mink, fishers, and black bears. But perhaps what's most noticeable about the taiga, at least if you're roaming these forests at night, are the owls. Boreal owls, great horned owls, hawk owls, great gray owls, barred owls, long-eared owls, northern hawk owls and in winter, snowy owls, all hunt in these forests. Like other predators in winter, owls can have a tough time catching prey animals, many of which are hidden under snow. Nevertheless, weasels, owls, and other species are sometimes able to hear or see animals under the snow. Weasels may dive down into the snow to grab a vole from its snug undersnow tunnel. And when a squirrel peeks out of its winter den for a breath

Little is known about wolverines, which live in taiga wilderness but are rarely seen.

· WOLVES: FAMILIES IN THE WILD ·

The big bad wolves of fairy tale fame are a far cry from real wolves. In the wild, these predators live a gentle family life, relying on a complex set of signals to hold their society together. Tail positions, facial expressions, body postures, barks, whines, and howls are all used by wolves to "talk" to one another. Communication is especially important because wolves live in packs—usually extended families—of 5 to 8 individuals. Groups often hunt together to bring down large animals such as caribou or moose. Wolf family members (aunts or cousins) may help care for the young while the other adults are out hunting.

In the taiga, wolves hunt caribou, bison, deer, beaver, and other animals. In the case of caribou and moose, wolves are generally able to catch only animals that are injured, weak, or sick. In this way, wolves help maintain the health of the prey population. Prey animals that are sick or deformed do not live to reproduce.

All domesticated dogs are descendants of wolves that were tamed. Although some people fear them, wild wolves are virtually harmless to humans. There is only one record of an attack by a wild wolf on a human. That occurred in 1942; it is suspected that the wolf was rabid, and was not behaving normally.

People's livestock and pets, however, *are* vulnerable to wolf attack. Ranchers who live near wolf territories may have their sheep or cattle attacked by wolves. Currently, the United States Fish and Wildlife Service has a program to control "problem" wolves that attack ranch animals. A conservation group has donated money to reimburse ranchers for animals lost to wolves. In North America, wolves are most plentiful in Canada and Alaska. In the lower 48 states wolves live in Minnesota; Wisconsin; Isle Royale, Michigan; and a few other scattered spots. Plans to reintroduce wolves to Yellowstone National Park in Montana are now underway.

of fresh air, a hungry hawk owl may glide down from its spruce tree perch and make that squirrel a meal.

FACING THE CHALLENGES OF WINTER

Even with all their adaptations, many taiga animals die in winter from starvation, frostbite, and hypothermia. Spring thaw can be dangerous as well, because melting snow swells streams that pour into animals' underground dens. In some particularly cold years, bird populations may move farther south than usual for the winter. Or the bulk of a particular animal population may die off in an unusually frigid winter. However, most taiga species, whose populations are small in spring, reproduce and successfully restock their species before the next winter. It is only in this way that these species could survive in the taiga year after year.

6
TAIGA COMMUNITIES

Strangely enough, trees can get sunburned. If a tree is adapted to living in the shade and the trees that normally shade it are suddenly cut down, the remaining tree may get sunburned. Its bark may actually turn red, blister, and fall off. This makes the tree's inner tissues more vulnerable to insect attack.

Protection from sun is only one of the ways a tree is affected by other plants nearby. A tree's life is connected to the lives of animals, too, such as the sawfly larvae that feed on its leaves, and the shrews that eat the cocoons of the sawfly larvae that eat its leaves. Shrews make such a difference in the life of trees that foresters sometimes release additional shrews into an area to kill off sawflies endangering valuable trees!

As these examples demonstrate, plants and animals in a community affect each others' lives in sometimes complex ways. Over thousands of years, they have adapted to one another, forming communities that are interwoven in a manner scientists are only beginning to understand.

GO WITH THE FLOW

The network of plants and animals in a community is held together, at least in part, by energy flow. In the taiga, for instance, energy in the form of sunlight is used by an evergreen tree to make sugars, which are stored as starch in its leaves, roots, shoots, and seed cones. When a snowshoe hare reaches up and nibbles evergreen leaves, part of the energy in those leaves becomes part of the hare. But some of that energy is also lost in the process, dissipated as heat, as it is every time energy is transferred from one organism to another. When a lynx chases down that snowshoe hare and eats it, the lynx gains part of the hare's energy. But once again, part of that energy is lost in the process.

Rotten Stuff When the lynx dies, scavengers such as ravens eat its body, and a portion of the lynx's energy becomes part of them. Decomposers—worms, bacteria, fungi, and small insects—eat the rest. The leftovers and by-products of decomposers' meals become part of the soil, which grows new evergreen trees. And so the energy flows through the community, continually replenished by energy from the sun.

In warm biomes, such as the tropics, decomposition of plants and animals can happen quickly. But decomposition occurs very slowly in the taiga, partly because it is cold there for much of the year. Leaf litter in the rain forest decomposes 60 times faster than leaf litter in the taiga! It takes three to five years for just one-half of the leaf litter on the floor of the taiga to decompose.

Organic matter—moss, fallen trees, tree leaves, branches, and so on—builds up on the taiga's forest floor. It will stay there, year after year, unless a fire sweeps through and clears it out. Much of this material is broken down and becomes part of the moss, or is trapped in the moss on the forest floor. These nutrients, trapped in mosses, are unavailable to the trees and other plants in the forest. At some places in the forest, moss—living and dead—may be 12 inches (30 centimeters) or more deep.

Energetic Ideas   A simple diagram of energy links such as the ones described above is called a food chain. Several food chains linked together create a food web—a diagram ecologists use to show the energy relationships between many organisms in a community. All the energy in a food web comes originally from sunlight. But because of its position on the earth, the taiga receives less natural energy—in the form of sunlight—than biomes closer to the equator. So the food chains and food webs of the taiga operate with less energy flowing through them than in many other biomes.

THE MEASURES OF LIFE

If you took all the plants in a square mile of taiga and piled them up on a scale, how much would they all weigh? It's hard to say. Yet this is the kind of thing ecologists try to measure, at least for small areas. The weight of plant matter—roots, shoots, and so on—for a certain area is called plant biomass. The taiga has 5 to 12 pounds per square foot (20 to 50 kilograms per square meter) of plant biomass, which is close to that of a temperate deciduous forest. Taiga, however, doesn't produce as much plant matter each year as does a temperate deciduous forest. Taiga justs "holds on" to more of its biomass—its leaves, for instance—year after year.

Diversity   Another important measure of a biome is species diversity. Species diversity is how many different kinds of organisms live in a place. Compared to tropical rain forests, deserts, grasslands, and deciduous forests, the species diversity of the taiga is low. For hundreds of miles, there may be only three or four tree species intermixed. Shrubs, mosses and lichens vary more. But the number of animal species is also low. Amphibian and reptile species are relatively scarce, although large mammal species are plentiful, as are birds. Overall, the taiga lacks the variety of life of biomes such as the tropical rain forest and temperate deciduous forest.

*Snowshoe hare populations go through a cycle, rising
and falling every few years.*

BOOM OR BUST: POPULATION CYCLES

In some years, snowshoe hares are abundant in the taiga.
During other years, they're not. Much of the evidence for
these population fluctuations comes from hunting and trapping records made in the early 1800s. Records show that
every ten years or so, the hare population "crashes." Soon
after, lynxes and other predators that eat hares decrease in
number as well. The reason the snowshoe hare population
crashes in the first place probably has to do with their over-
grazing of habitat. But overcrowding, weather, predation,
fire, and disease also play a role in the population size of
snowshoe hares, and of many predators, as well. For what-
ever reason, the taiga populations of owls, hares, grouse,
lynx, and other animals rise and fall every few years.

BEFORE AND AFTER FIRE

The taiga's history is tied to fire. Even though it's a generally moist biome, parts of it, particularly in Alaska, northwest Canada, and central Siberia, can be quite dry at times. Lightning can easily spark a fire in the waxy, dry needles on the forest floor, causing a fire that burns millions of forest acres. People also cause fires by setting them to clear land, or accidentally, with stray sparks from a campfire or a discarded cigarette.

Succession   What regrows after a fire depends on how severely a forest is burned. However, there is a general order to the taiga's regrowth. After a devastating fire, quick-sprouting meadow plants move in first. These species, in turn, create conditions in which broadleaf, deciduous trees such as birch and aspen can thrive. Later, under the shelter of these broadleaf trees, conifers such as spruce and fir can grow. Eventually they surpass the broadleaf trees and shade them out. This process, when one type of plant/animal community takes the place of another, is called succession. Succession generally leads to a "climax community" that will last until another disturbance occurs.

A Cycle of Disturbance   It may take several hundred years, but a spruce-fir community usually regrows on burned areas. But most scientists don't call it a "climax" forest because they're not sure if these forests would last in this stage forever. In some places, forests become bogs, because moss builds up so much it insulates the ground. This keeps the ground so cold it doesn't thaw enough in summer for trees to thrive. Few forests reach this point, however, because fires, logging, and shifting stream beds disturb the forests' successional pattern.

A Part of the Process   Succession isn't good or bad; it's part of a natural process of change. After a fire, in the new habitat created by the fire, conditions are good for some animals and plants and bad for others. Bears, for instance, seem to prefer forests with more deciduous trees. In these forests, they can take advantage of both the abundant food of the deciduous trees and the secure shelter of the spruce forests.

BOGS, MUSKEGS, AND OTHER SQUISHY SPOTS
Step onto a bog and you'll feel the mossy ground squish and shake underfoot. It feels like standing on top of a waterbed or gently bouncing on a trampoline. But what you're actually standing on is a very thick layer of moss overlying what was once a pond. These bogs can be found scattered in the taiga forests.

Bog Formation   The most common way bogs form is when plants at the edge of a pond grow out and over the water. Plant parts fill in the pool. Sphagnum moss, cottongrass, orchids, pitcher plants, and other plants fill in the wet areas. Eventually, shrubs such as Labrador tea can become established. The now shrubby land dries out and eventually trees can grow on it. Then the bog becomes a muskeg, a wetland where trees grow. Later, the muskeg may fill up entirely, until there is no water left.

Sphagnum moss can build up in bogs for thousands of years, creating a layer of moss meters deep. Peat bogs are so acidic that the bacteria that normally decompose dead plants and animals do not thrive there. As a result, scientists can study pollen grains trapped in the lower layers of bogs to find out about the plants that lived there long ago. In European bogs, scientists have discovered the well-preserved remains of humans who lived thousands of years ago.

For Peat's Sake   The moss of boreal bogs is often harvested and sold as peat moss, which people use in their gardens.

Peat is also used as a fuel in many countries. The slow, long-lasting burn of peat makes fires in the taiga especially persistent. In Alaska, a raging summer forest fire that seemed to have died out in the winter returned the next summer. It had survived the winter, smoldering in the deep layers of peat.

THE STORY OF A YOUNG BIOME

In its current position, the taiga is a fairly recent development. During the last ice age, glaciers covered much of the land where the taiga is today, except for parts of interior Alaska and portions of Canada. South of the ice, in places such as southern Illinois, Georgia, and Kansas, a taiga forest grew where no taiga grows naturally today. Then, as the earth warmed and the ice caps melted and shrank, those previously glaciated areas of Canada and Alaska were uncovered. First tundra plants and later taiga plants spread over the newly revealed ground. The taiga plants that colonized these lands had existed in unglaciated areas. Climatic changes caused prairie and temperate deciduous forest to move into areas that had previously been taiga.

TAKE A HIKE IN THE TAIGA

If you take a daytime hike in the taiga, don't forget to bring warm clothes, a light jacket in summer, and many warm layers in winter. Know where you're going, tell someone of your plans, and bring a map. Carry enough water and enough food to keep your energy levels high. Long pants and a long-sleeved shirt can help prevent mosquito and other bug bites. Bug repellent can help, too.

Here are just a few of the things you can look for, smell for, and listen for on a taiga hike:

- The grating trill of a red squirrel;
- A tree cavity where woodpeckers nest;

- Wolf tracks in the snow;
- A red fox den under tree roots near a riverbank;
- Piles of cone scales a squirrel has dropped from a perch above;
- Gnaw marks of porcupines on trees;
- Egg-shaped, brown droppings of moose;
- Claw marks of brown bears on trees;
- Pungent smell of spruce tree resin;
- Cone-shaped stumps left by a beaver's gnawing;
- A beaver lodge (smaller lodges belong to muskrat);
- Quaking bogs, where mossy ground shakes underfoot.

TAIGA LOOK-ALIKE

If you climb a mountain in Arizona, or Colorado, or Vermont, you may walk through a forest of conifers that looks something like taiga. That's because by climbing a mountain, you can reach altitudes where the weather is cool and the soil is thin. These mountainsides have climatic conditions that are somewhat similar to those of places hundreds, even thousands, of miles north. Conifer forests near the timberline often look much like the taiga. While these woodlands aren't exactly like the taiga in structure or species present, they often have much in common ecologically.

If you keep climbing up such a mountain, to beyond where trees grow, you may reach fields of low-growing plants called alpine tundra. Alpine tundra has much in common with Arctic tundra, the biome that grows north of the taiga. Once again, the climatic effects of altitude enable some of the same species and types of animals to survive in both these areas. That's the magic of the mountains!

7
PEOPLE AND THE TAIGA

Great expanses of the boreal forest—the taiga—remain wild. Yet as human population rises, demand for energy and products increases. The push to harvest the taiga's natural resources grows ever stronger. Dam building, mining, peat moss harvesting, road building, logging, fishing, and hunting all can take a toll on the taiga and its wildlife. Air pollution, ozone depletion, and global climate change can also affect this biome. Because of these factors, the future survival of the large tracts of undeveloped land that now exist in the taiga is in question.

ANCIENT TAIGA PEOPLE

Sometime in the last 15,000 to 40,000 years, the first people came to North America. They crossed over the Bering Land Bridge, which once connected what is now Alaska with what is now Russia. This 1,000-mile- (1,600-kilometer-) wide land bridge existed several times in the past 40,000 years, whenever the climate was cold enough to lock up much of the ocean's water in ice, thereby lowering the seas and exposing the land.

Today many of the Native Americans that live in the taiga are descended from the Athabascans, the first people to come over the Bering Strait. There are many Inuit, as well—also called Eskimo—who are descended from people who crossed over the Bering Strait thousands of years later. Although cultural practices vary, the hunting and gather-

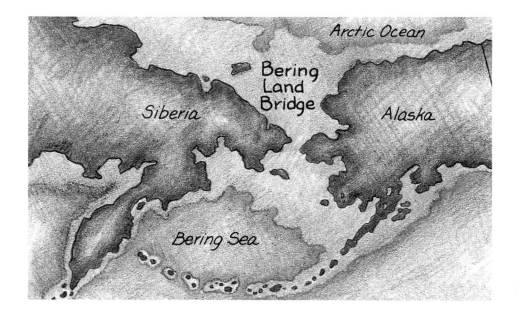

The regions of Siberia and Alaska once connected by a land bridge are now called Beringia.

ing traditions of these native people are quite similar. Most harvest berries and herbs, fish for salmon, and hunt and trap arctic hares, moose, weasels, bears, muskrats, beavers, and other animals.

Ingenious Invention   Over the years, taiga people have developed ingenious ways of solving the challenges of forest living. Athabascan hunters sometimes build a *quin-zhee*, a temporary snow house, when they are out hunting. They shovel snow into a pile, let it set for an hour or so, then tunnel into it, excavating a hollow, cavelike home. With the help of body heat, such a snow house can be up to 25°F (14°C) warmer than the outside air.

Animals and plants are used in a wide variety of ways, too. Consider tree sap, for instance. This sticky sap protects a tree by plugging cracks in its bark so insects and plant diseases cannot get inside. Native people used this sap to plug

• TOP HATS AND TAILS •

Back in the 1700s, tophats were daily wear for the high fashion folks of Europe. And that was bad news for animals with real tails: beavers. That's because the tighly woven, woolly underfur of the beaver was the material made into felt to construct these hats.

Top hats were so popular that demand for beaver pelts was a major factor in the exploration and settlement of the taiga by European Americans. Trapping was big business in the 1700s in Canada and the United States. Marten, mink, muskrat, lynx, wolverine, bear, and ermine furs were also harvested. Meat from these animals was eaten as well. In one year, the skins of 127,080 beavers and 16,512 bears were shipped from Canada through just one French port.

In the early days, most furs were obtained from Native Americans, who swapped them for other goods. But as demand increased, French-Canadian and British trappers traveled far back into the forest, paddling canoes along lakes and streams, to harvest beavers. At that time, beavers were plentiful. By the early 1800s, beavers were rare or even absent from most areas where they were once common. Today, with some protection, beavers are slowly increasing in number. Trapping of beavers is now regulated by law.

holes, too—in their birch bark canoes. Hardened white spruce sap was also chewed as gum. And it was used to help heal cuts. These are just a few of the ingenious uses taiga people have made of forest products—from moose skin mattresses to caribou hide boots to spruce needle medicines.

FUR COUNTRIES

For thousands of years, the lives of the Athabascan and Inuit remained virtually unchanged. But in the early 1700s, French explorers began moving into the taiga from what is now the eastern coast of Canada and the northeastern United States. These people were trappers, looking for animal pelts to take back to Europe. In the late 1800s, people came from all over to the taiga in search of gold. In Canada and parts of Alaska, towns were created almost overnight to house the gold seekers. They brought not only new technologies, but also liquor and other drugs, gambling, and disease. Many natives died from direct conflict with European settlers, but even more died from diseases such as smallpox, brought by settlers.

PEOPLE IN THE TAIGA TODAY

Native people who inhabit the taiga live a lifestyle that is a combination of old and new. In many Alaskan villages, people's lives are still closely linked to the seasons. In those areas, people survive largely by hunting or trapping. But in bigger towns and cities, most residents are of nonnative descent. People rely on the tourist trade and modern industry to survive. Farming is rare because farming on a large scale is not very practical in the taiga's shallow, acidic, often nutrient-poor soils.

ACID RAIN AND DYING LAKES

In Germany, Czechoslovakia, and other parts of northern Europe, forests are dying. Thousands of acres of taiga have already died there, leaving gray, needleless trees, like eerie skeletons. In North America, forests in New England and eastern Canada are showing symptoms of trouble, too. Many scientists suspect this tree damage is caused by acid rain—rain and snow acidified by contact with pollutants in the air. These pollutants come from coal-burning power plants and other factories, but also volcanoes as well.

Over the years, the rain in many areas of the world has become more acid. At the same time, trees have been dying off in huge numbers, especially at high altitudes, where

Evergreen trees in the taiga show the devastating effects of acid rain.

trees are often bathed in acidic fog. Scientists believe that acid rain stresses trees, weakening them so they have little resistance to disease, cold winters, insect attacks, and other direct causes of death. But the evidence that directly links tree damage to acid rain is still not clear-cut.

However, one proven result of acid rain is the death of fish and other animals that live in lakes. Since the 1950s, thousands of lakes in Sweden and Norway have become sterile—lifeless. Trout and other organisms in these lakes have died. These fish kills occur most often when acid snow melts in spring, flushing acidic water into streams, lakes, and rivers.

Acid rain also causes additional problems. When the acid washes through the soil, it releases naturally occurring minerals. Once released from the soil, these minerals can build up—sometimes to poisonous levels—in plants and animals. Some areas have alkaline soils, which help neutralize acidic water that flows over them. But most taiga soils are acidic to begin with, so they can't neutralize the acidic water. Plants that live in these soils are especially vulnerable to damage from acid rain.

ACID RAIN TEST

Do you live in an area where acid rain falls? You can find out for yourself.

Here are the materials you will need:
- Six to ten wide-mouth jars with caps (one for each area where you will be gathering samples)
- pH test paper (It's best to get paper with a wide range, pH 1-12. You can order it from Carolina Biological Supply, phone: 1- 800-334-5555. Paper or test kits may be available from other biological supply companies, from gardening stores, pet stores, etc.)
- One gallon (3.8 liters) distilled water
- Color key for pH paper (usually comes with pH paper)
- Tweezers for handling pH paper

Scientists measure relative acidity using pH. It works on a scale of 0-14, with 7 being neutral. Readings below 7 are acid, and readings above 7 are alkaline, the opposite of acid. The scale is logarithmic, meaning pH 5 is 10 times more acid than pH 6, and pH 4 is 100 times more acid than pH 6.

Wash all the jars thoroughly. Rinse them in distilled water, making sure there are no residues of soap or other materials inside. Then cap them tightly until ready for use. (Don't touch the insides or rims of the jars after rinsing, because that can change your results.) Decide on six or more sites where you will gather rainwater. You might arrange with friends who live in other neighborhoods to collect rain in their area. Open a jar and set it outside during rain to collect a rainwater sample. Cap the jar as soon as the sample has been collected. (You only need a few tablespoons of rain at most). Label each jar with the location and time the sample was collected.

As soon as possible, test the rain samples for acidity. Using the tweezers, dip a piece of pH paper about 2 inches (5 centimeters) long in the water. Let it sit in the water for about a minute. Then take it out and compare its color to those on the color key. That will tell you the relative acidity of the sample. Record all the readings.

What was the average reading for acidity in your area? Normal rain is generally about pH 5.7. But it can vary. Anything lower than 5.7 is somewhat acidic rain. Fish die in lakes with acidity as low as 4.5. Lemon juice, which is very acid, is around pH 2.2.

Your class may want to join the National Geographic Society's Kidsnet, a computer-based acid rain testing network. For information, contact:

National Geographic Society
Attention: Educational Services
P.O. Box 98018
Washington, DC 20090
Phone 1-800-368-2728

DAMS: A MAJOR ISSUE

With its many rivers and few people, the taiga is seen as a good place for hydroelectric dams. By harnessing the power of water, a hydroelectric dam produces electricity without creating the air pollution that coal and petroleum burning factories do. And dams don't pose the danger of releasing harmful radioactive gases, as do nuclear power plants. But hydroelectric dams have other large-scale, damaging effects on the environment.

When a river is dammed to produce power, a gigantic lake backs up behind it. Dams can flood thousands of acres of land, killing wildlife and permanently displacing people from their homes. Dams and channels change the flow of the rivers and block the migration of salmon and other animals.

In the taiga of Quebec, Canada, the largest hydroelectric project in the world—the James Bay Project—is underway. Already, project construction has flooded 4,000 square miles (10,360 square kilometers) of land, changed the course of a major river, and led to the death of 10,000 caribou. Increased water flow has already released mercury from the region's soil, poisoning some fish and the people who eat them. This hydroelectric project is also displacing the Cree people from their native lands.

Future plans involve flooding thousands more square miles of land, building several hundred dams, channeling 19 major rivers, and destroying large areas of taiga for facilities to house the people and equipment needed to run the project.

OTHER CONSERVATION THREATS
TO THE TAIGA

Hydroelectric projects and acid rain are not the only conservation threats to the taiga. Other activities, such as timbering, have a significant effect on the taiga as well. Here's the rundown on some of those threats:

Timber Harvest   In North America, timber harvest is only beginning to become common in the taiga. In Scandinavian countries, however, timber harvest has had a major impact on the taiga.

Air Pollution in General   Air pollution from cars, wood burning, factories, and other sources can be an especially difficult problem in northern areas such as the taiga.

Temperature inversions, which often occur in winter, trap pollution from local sources close to the ground. This pollution can concentrate, forming a dense, dangerous fog that can last for hours or days.

Development   Like all other biomes, unwise development could spoil the taiga. Land is being cleared for housing, ski slopes, landfills, new roads, and other facilities. Future development could put portions of the taiga and some of its wildlife populations in jeopardy. Habitat loss, and habitat degradation because of pollution or fragmentation of areas into small, disconnected tracts are both potential problems.

Mining   Mining for aluminum and other minerals is widespread in taiga regions. Chemicals used in mining and silt released by mining operations can contaminate streams, and the process as a whole can leave scars upon the land. A less well-known type of mining—peat mining—harvests peat moss for fuel and for sale to gardeners. This destroys bog habitats.

Overharvesting of Wildlife   The meat gained from hunting, trapping, and fishing is the mainstay of the diet of many native people and recent immigrants to the taiga. Today, guns, powerboats, planes, and snowmobiles make hunting and trapping easier. And many more people come to the taiga to fish and hunt for recreation. Some wildlife managers believe more restrictive regulations on hunting and trapping may be needed, especially where wildlife populations are already in danger because of environmental problems.

Ozone Depletion   Chlorofluorocarbons (CFCs) and other chemicals people use to make aerosol foam and to run refrigerators are destroying the ozone layer, a thin layer of ozone gas surrounding the earth. This layer shields the

Snowmobiles and other technological advances have affected how hunting and trapping are carried out in the taiga.

earth and its inhabitants from harmful ultraviolet rays that cause skin cancer. As the ozone layer thins, ultraviolet radiation will increase, and it is unknown what effect increased ultraviolet radiation will have on people, plants, and animals of the taiga.

Greenhouse Effect   Greenhouse gases, which occur naturally in the earth's atmosphere, keep the earth warm. These gases act like the glass panes of a greenhouse, allowing sunlight to enter the earth's atmosphere while allowing only some of the sunlight-generated heat to escape. That's fine. But today, people's activities, such as cattle ranching, industry, the running of automobiles, and the burning of tropical forests, have increased the amount of greenhouse gas in the atmosphere. Scientists aren't sure how this increased greenhouse gas will affect the world's climate. Some suspect the earth's climate may warm, causing the snow cover to melt and thawing some of the permafrost. This could cause taiga to spread northward. But no one is really certain what will happen; the effects of such global atmospheric changes are hard to predict.

HOPE FOR THE FUTURE

Despite the problems facing the taiga, there's plenty of hope for the future. Consider what some people are doing to safeguard the taiga biome:

- In Sweden, the Taiga Rescue Network educates consumers about the timber cutting occurring in the taiga. They encourage people to conserve wood products—from toilet paper to furniture—that are made from taiga trees.
- The Cree people have written letters, filed court cases, and staged demonstrations to oppose the James Bay hydroelectric project. Their efforts have caused some delays in the project, but have been unsuccessful in changing the overall plans. They continue to protest the project.
- In 1993 the Canadian government, working with Native Indian groups, established a new taiga park, Vuntut National Park, in the Yukon Territory.
- Activists from a variety of groups are trying to convince the state of Alaska to cancel its plans to start a large-scale road building project. There is concern that building these roads through many wild areas of Alaska will damage habitat and bring in hunters where animal populations were previously untouched.

These actions are just a small sampling of what's going on in taiga regions. Fortunately, the taiga, at least in North America, is less damaged than many other biomes. Environmental activists believe that if people take notice of conservation threats now, with careful and sensible planning the future for the taiga will be bright. But more people are needed to lend a helping hand in these conservation efforts. You can get involved, too!

RESOURCES AND WHAT
YOU CAN DO TO HELP

Here's what you can do to help ensure that taigas are conserved:

• Learn more by reading books and watching videos and television programs about the taiga. Check your local library, bookstore, and video store for resources. Here are just a few of the books available for further reading:

A Field Guide to the Ecology of Western Forests by John C. Kricher (Peterson Field Guide Series) (Houghton Mifflin, 1993).

"Of Waterhens and Wood Bison," *International Wildlife* (May/June 1988).

"Peoples of the Arctic," *National Geographic* (February 1983).

Winter, An Ecological Handbook by James C. Halfpenny and Roy Douglas Ozanne (Johnson Books, 1989).

The World of Northern Evergreens by E. C. Pielou (Cornell University Press, 1988).

• For more information on taiga and taiga-related issues, get in touch with the following organizations:

Audubon Society
Alaska Regional Office
308 G Street #217
Anchorage, AK 99501
Phone 1-907-276-7034

Wilderness Society
Regional Office
430 West 7th Avenue
Suite 210
Anchorage, AK 99501-3550
Phone 1-907-272-9453

Northern Alaska
Environmental Center
218 Driveway
Fairbanks, AK 99701
Phone 1-907-452-5021

If you like the job these organizations are doing, consider becoming a member.

• To order taiga-related books, posters, and other materials, contact these companies and ask for information on their taiga products:

Alaska Geographic Society
P. O. Box 93370
Anchorage, AK 99509-3370
Phone 1-907-562-0164
(They publish a magazine
and maps.)

Alaska Northwest
Publishing Company
130 Second Avenue South
Edmonds, WA 98020
Phone 1-206-774-9009
(They publish books, maps,
and magazines. Ask for
their catalog.)

• Visit a museum, national park, or botanical garden that has taiga features or displays. The following North American parks, refuges, forests, and preserves contain taiga:

Canada
Gros Mourne National Park, Rocky Harbor,
    Newfoundland

Ivvavik (North Yukon National Park), Inuvik, NT
Vuntut National Park, Dawson City, Yukon Territory
Wood Buffalo National Park, Fort Smith, NT

United States
Chugach National Forest, Anchorage, AK
Denali National Park and Preserve, McKinley Park, AK
Gates of the Arctic National Park, Bettles, AK
Isle Royale National Park, Houghton, MI
Voyageurs National Park, International Falls, MN
Yukon-Charley Rivers National Preserve, Eagle, AK

• Turn off lights, televisions, and other appliances when you are not using them. Saving electricity can prevent the need for hydroelectric plants that generate it. (Building dams for hydroelectric plants floods large areas of the taiga.) For energy-saving tips, contact your local electric utility. For a catalog of energy-saving appliances and other environmental products, write or call:

Real Goods
966 Mazzoni Street
Ukiah, CA 95482-3471
Phone 1-800-762-7325

Seventh Generation
Colchester, Vermont
05446-1672
Phone 1-800-456-1177

• Educate others about the taiga and taiga peoples. Put on a skit at school, construct a display for the hall or a mall to raise awareness of taiga issues.

• Get to know young people who live on the taiga or near it. For pen pal information, write or call the following for applications. Be sure to mention you're interested in exchanging letters with young people in Scandinavia, Russia, Greenland, Canada, Alaska, or other taiga regions.

Student Letter Exchange
630 Third Avenue
New York, NY 10017
Phone 1-212-557-3312

• Write letters to state and national government officials, telling them you feel taiga—boreal forest—conservation is important. Make suggestions for what they could do to help conserve taiga.

• Reduce your consumption of products, reuse what products you can. Recycle aluminum cans, paper, plastic, and other products. Recycling uses less energy than making a product from scratch. Also, buy recycled products.

GLOSSARY

acid rain   general term for precipitation that has been acid-ified by pollution in the air

biome   an area that has a certain kind of climate and a certain kind of community of plants and animals

boreal forest   taiga

climax community   a community whose composition—ratio of plant species—does not change significantly over time. A climax community is the final stage in succession.

closed forest   taiga that has trees close together and a shaded, often moss-covered forest floor

conifer   a tree that bears cones, such as pine cones

deciduous   plants that drop all their leaves each year

ecotone   a border between two biomes, where the plants and animals of those biomes mix

evergreen   plants that keep their leaves for more than one year

food chain   a simplified diagram showing the transfer of energy from the sun to a plant, from that plant to a plant eater, from the plant eater to a meat eater, and so on

food web   a diagram that shows energy flow in a community by showing how the food chains in that community are linked

glacier   a large river of ice that spreads out over land

hardening   the process by which a plant changes its internal chemistry during winter to avoid frost and damage from freezing

hibernation   an animal's sluggish state of reduced metabolism and reduced body temperature that helps it survive winter

isotherm   an imaginary line that bounds an area where certain temperatures occur

layering   a process by which a tree branch becomes partly covered in soil and consequently forms roots. This branch can then grow into a tree separate from the parent plant.

lichen   a living structure created by the partnership between an alga and a fungus. The alga and fungus together function as if they are one organism, when in fact they are not.

lichen woodland   taiga that has trees spaced far apart, with lichen growing in between them

microclimate   the environmental conditions in a small habitat, or at a particular site

permafrost   frozen ground

plant biomass   the weight of all the plant matter—roots, shoots, stems, and other plant parts—for a given area

podzol   a layered soil common in coniferous forests

species diversity   the number of different kinds of plants, animals, and other organisms in a given area

succession   the process by which a sequence of plant communities replace one another in a given area

taiga   a biome that is characterized by severe winters, persistent snow cover, and conifers such as spruce, fir, and tamarack. Taiga, also called the boreal forest or northern coniferous forest, occurs south of the tundra and north of temperate grasslands and temperate deciduous forest.

INDEX